Your Personal Food Truck Experience

Some of the most Popular Food Truck

Recipes in one Place

BY: SOPHIA FREEMAN

Liability

This publication is meant as an informational tool. The individual purchaser accepts all liability if damages occur because of following the directions or guidelines set out in this publication. The Author bears no responsibility for reparations caused by the misuse or misinterpretation of the content.

Copyright

My gift to you!

Thank you, cherished reader, for purchasing my book and taking the time to read it. As a special reward for your decision, I would like to offer a gift of free and discounted books directly to your inbox. All you need to do is fill in the box below with your email address and name to start getting amazing offers in the comfort of your own home. You will never miss an offer because a reminder will be sent to you. Never miss a deal and get great deals without having to leave the house! Subscribe now and start saving!

Subscribe to the Newsletter!

Your email address | Subscribe

Table of Contents

Delicious Food Truck Recipes

zzzzzzzzzzzzzzzzzzzzzzzzzzzzzzzzzzzzzzzzzzzzzzzzzzzzzzz

1) Cheesesteak Style Pizza

This is the perfect pizza dish to make during your next pizza night. Topped off with authentic cheesesteak and green bell peppers, this is a filling pizza dish with a bit of a kick to it.

Serving Size: 8 Servings

Preparation Time: 1 Hour and 50 Minutes

Ingredient List:

- 2 ¼ teaspoons of Yeast, Active and Dry
- 1 Cup of Water, Lukewarm Variety
- 1 tablespoon of Honey, Raw
- 2 ¼ to 2 ½ Cups of Flour, All-Purpose Variety
- 1 teaspoon of Salt, For Taste
- ½ teaspoons of Garlic, Powdered Variety
- 1 teaspoon of Oregano Flakes, Dried
- 2 Tablespoons of Olive Oil, Extra Virgin Variety and Evenly Divided
- ½ of an Onion, Thinly Sliced
- ½ of a Bell Pepper, Green in Color
- 2 Cheesecake Patties, Broken Apart
- 1 tablespoon of Worcestershire Sauce
- 2 Tablespoons of Steak Sauce
- 1, 8 Ounce Jar of Pizza Sauce, White in Color
- 6 to 8 Slices of Provolone Cheese, Thinly Sliced

ZZZZZZZZZZZZZZZZZZZZZZZZZZZZZZZZZZZZZZZZZZZZZZZZZZZZZZZZZZZ

Instructions:

1. First use a large sized bowl and add in your raw honey and active yeast. Stir thoroughly to combine and set aside to sit for the next 7 to 10 minutes or until your mixture is foamy.

2. After this time add in your all-purpose flour, powdered garlic and dried oregano. Stir thoroughly to combine before drizzling in at least one spoonful of your olive oil. Stir to incorporate until a dough begins to form.

3. Place your dough onto a lightly floured surface. Knead for the next 10 minutes or until your dough is soft to the touch. Place your dough into a lightly greased bowl and wrap with some plastic wrap. Allow to sit for the next hour or until your dough has doubled in size.

4. After this time, preheat your oven to 425 degrees. Then place a large sized skillet over medium to high heat. Add another spoonful of your olive oil into your skillet and swirl around to coat. Once your oil is hot enough add in your chopped onions and bell peppers. Cook for the next 5 to 7 minutes or until your mixture is tender to the touch.

5. Push your veggies to the side of your skillet and add in your steak patties. Season with some Worcestershire sauce and steak sauce. Cook according to the direction on the package until full cooked through. Remove from heat and set aside for later use.

6. Place your dough onto a lightly floured surface and divide into two pieces. Roll both of your portions of dough into even sized discs.

7. Place your pizza dough onto a pizza sheet lined with a sheet of parchment paper. Spoon your sauce over your pizza dough, making sure to leave at least ½ an inch border around the edges. Sprinkle your onion, pepper and steak mixture over the top.

8. Tear your cheese slices in half and place over your meat mixture.

9. Place your pizza into your oven to bake for the next 10 to 13 minutes or until the edges are golden brown in color and your cheese is beginning to turn brown in color.

10. Remove and allow to cool for the next 5 minutes before slicing.

2) Delicious Fried Calamari Sandwich

This is yet another savory seafood food truck recipe I know you are going to fall in love with the moment you get a bite of it yourself. Topped with some fiery Sriracha sauce and fresh herbs, this is one fish that will become a family favorite in your household.

Serving Size: 2 Servings

Preparation Time: 20 Minutes

Ingredient List:

- ½ Cup of Mayonnaise, Your Favorite Kind
- 1 tablespoon of Sriracha Sauce
- 1 teaspoon of Red Chile Flakes, Crushed
- 1 tablespoon of Oil, Canola Variety and Extra for Frying
- 2 Cloves of Garlic, Sliced Thinly
- 2 teaspoons of Fish Sauce
- 6 Chiles de Arbol, Dried, Stemmed, Soaked and Drained
- 1 Pound of Calamari Rings and Tentacles, Fully Cleaned
- 2 Cups of Cornmeal
- 2, Hoagie Rolls, 6 Inches in Length and Soft to the Touch
- 6 Basil Leaves, Fresh
- 4 Sprigs of Cilantro, Fresh and Roughly Chopped
- ¼ of a Cucumber, Sliced Thinly
- ¼ Bulb of Fennel, Sliced Thinly
- 1 Lime, Fresh, Peeled and Cut into Segments

zzzzzzzzzzzzzzzzzzzzzzzzzzzzzzzzzzzzzzzzzzzzzzzzzzzzzzzzzzzz

Instructions:

1. Use a small sized bowl and add in your favorite kind of mayonnaise, sriracha sauce and chile flakes. Stir thoroughly to combine and set this mixture aside for later use.

2. Next, place a medium sized saucepan over medium to high heat. Add in your oil and once your oil is hot enough add in your garlic. Cook for at least one minute or until fragrant. Then add in your fish sauce and chiles de arbol. Continue to cook for the next 3 minutes or until tender to the touch. Remove and transfer into a bowl. Set aside for later use.

3. Place a large sized Dutch oven over medium to high heat. Pour into at least two inches of oil and heat until it reaches 360 degrees.

4. While your oil is heating up, dredge your calamari in your cornmeal, making sure to shake off the excess. Gently drop into your hot oil and fry for at least 2 to 3 minutes or until fully cooked through. Remove and place onto a plate lined with paper towels to drain.

5. Then assemble your sandwiches. To do this, split open your rolls. Spoon some of your mayonnaise mixture onto one side of your sandwich. Then add in your chiles, fresh basil, chopped cilantro, fresh cucumber slices, sliced fennel and cooked calamari. Top off with your fresh lime segments and bring your sandwich together. Serve right away and enjoy.

3) Cornbread Waffles with Chili

There is no other breakfast dish that is sure to warm you up then this perfect food truck recipe. Made with a sweet tasting waffle top off with filling and spicy chili, I know you will want to make this dish every morning.

Serving Size: 4 Servings

Preparation Time: 20 Minutes

Ingredient List:

- 1 ¾ Cups of Flour, All-Purpose Variety
- 1 ¼ Cups of Cornmeal, Yellow in Color
- 1 tablespoon of Baker's Style Baking Powder
- 1 teaspoon of Sugar, White in Color
- 1 teaspoon of Salt, For Taste
- 2 Cups of Milk, Whole
- 3 Tablespoons of Oil, Vegetable Variety
- 2 Eggs, Large in Size and Beaten Lightly
- 4 Cups of Chili, with Beans, Hot and Canned Variety
- Some Cheddar Cheese, Sharp, Finely Shredded and For Topping
- Some Sour Cream, For Topping
- Dash of Cilantro, Fresh, Roughly Chopped and For Garnish

zzzzzzzzzzzzzzzzzzzzzzzzzzzzzzzzzzzzzzzzzzzzzzzzzzzzzzzzz

Instructions:

1. The first thing that you will want to do is make your waffles. To do this, first preheat a waffle iron.

2. While your waffle iron is heating up, use a large sized bowl and add in your all-purpose flour, cornmeal, baker's style baking powder, white sugar and dash of salt. Stir thoroughly to combine.

3. Then add in your whole milk, vegetable oil and large eggs. Stir again until smooth in consistency.

4. Pour at least ¼ cup of your batter onto your hot waffle iron. Close the lid and allow to cook for at least 5 minutes or until golden in color.

5. Pour your hot chili over the top of your waffles.

6. Garnish your waffles with your shredded cheese, soft sour cream and fresh cilantro. Enjoy while piping hot.

4) Delicious Empanadas

Even if you aren't of Spanish descent, doesn't mean that you can't make this delicious empanada dish. Stuffed with hearty beef and fried to perfection, this is one empanada recipe I know you will want to make as often as possible.

Serving Size: 24 Servings

Preparation Time: 30 Minutes

Ingredient List:

- 1 ½ Pounds of Beef, lean and Ground
- 1 ½ Pounds of Onion, Sliced Thinly
- 2 Cloves of Garlic, Minced
- Half of a Bell Pepper, Red in Color and Finely Diced
- 1/3 Cup of Pimenton Dulce or Paprika for Taste
- ½ teaspoons of Cumin, Ground
- ½ teaspoons of Nutmeg, Ground
- Dash of Salt and Black Pepper, For Taste

Ingredients for Your Pastry:

- 6 Cups of Flour, All-Purpose Variety
- 1 1/3 Cups of Lard, Warm
- 1 teaspoon of Salt, For Taste
- 1 Cup of Water, Warm

ZZZZZZZZZZZZZZZZZZZZZZZZZZZZZZZZZZZZZZZZZZZZZZZZZZZZZZZ

Instructions:

1. First prepare your filling. To do this, place a large sized skillet over medium heat. Once your skillet is hot enough add in your ground beef. Cook for at least 30 to 40 minutes or until your beef is brown in color.

2. Then add in your diced onions, minced garlic and diced bell peppers. Continue to cook for another 10 to 15 minutes or until your veggies are soft to the touch. Season with a dash of salt and black pepper.

3. Transfer your filling into your fridge to chill for the next 6 to 8 hours or until cold to the touch.

4. During this time prepare your pastry. To do this use a large sized bowl and add in your flour and salt. Stir to combine before adding in your lard. Use your hands and mix until thoroughly incorporated. Add in your warm water and stir again to combine.

5. Transfer your dough onto a lightly floured surface and roll until at least 4 inches in diameter and at least ¼ inch in thickness. Cut your dough into even sized discs.

6. Place a spoonful or two of your filling directly into the center of each disc. Fold your dough over your filling and crimp the edges with a fork to seal. Place your assembled empanadas onto a large sized baking sheet lined with a sheet of parchment paper.

7. Fill a large sized pot with a generous amount of oil for frying. Set over medium heat and allow to come to 400 degrees. Once your oil is hot enough gently add in your empanadas. Fry for at least 5 to 7 minutes or until golden brown in color. Remove and place onto a plate lined with paper towels to drain. Repeat with your remaining empanadas until they have all been cooked. Serve whenever you are ready.

5) Korean Style BBQ Tacos

To start things off we have this delicious taco recipe that I know you will want to enjoy as often as possible. Packed full of marinated beef seared to perfection and topped with some garbage style slaw and cucumbers, this is one taco recipe I know you won't be able to get enough of.

Serving Size: 8 Servings

Preparation Time: 35 Minutes

Ingredients for Your Beef:

- 1 ¼ Pounds of Flank Steak, Sliced Thinly
- ¼ Cup of Soy Sauce, Your Favorite Kind
- 2 Tablespoons of Brown Sugar, Light and Packed
- 3 Cloves of Garlic, Minced
- 2 teaspoons of Ginger, Fresh and Minced
- ½ teaspoons of Chile Flakes, Red in Color and Optional
- Dash of Salt and Black Pepper, For Taste
- 2 teaspoons of Oil, Vegetable Variety

Ingredients for Your Slaw:

- 2 Cups of Cabbage, Green in Color and Finely Shredded
- 1 Cup of Cabbage, Purple in Color and Finely Shredded
- ½ Cup of Carrots, Fresh and Finely Shredded
- 1 tablespoon of Lime Juice, Fresh
- 1 tablespoon of Olive Oil, Extra Virgin Variety
- ¼ Cup of Green Onions, Sliced Thinly
- Dash of Salt and Black Pepper, For Taste

Ingredients for Your Pickled Cucumbers:

- 1 Cup of Cucumber, Fresh and Sliced Thinly
- 2 Tablespoons of Vinegar, Rice
- ½ teaspoons of Sugar, White in Color
- Dash of Salt, For Taste
- 8 Tortillas, Flour Variety and Small in Size

ZZZZZZZZZZZZZZZZZZZZZZZZZZZZZZZZZZZZZZZZZZZZZZZZZZZZZZZZ

Instructions:

1. Use a large sized Ziploc bag and add in your favorite kind of soy sauce, light brown sugar, minced garlic, minced ginger, red chile flakes if you are using it and a dash of salt and black pepper. Shake vigorously to combine and add in your flank steak. Shake again to coat. Allow your meat to marinate for the next 15 minutes.

2. During this time use a small sized bowl and add in your fresh cucumber, vinegar, white sugar and dash of salt. Stir thoroughly to combine. Cover with a sheet of plastic wrap and place into your fridge to chill for the next 15 minutes.

3. Then place a large sized skillet over high heat. Add in a touch of oil and once your oil is hot enough add in your flank steak. Cook for the next 4 to 5 minutes or until your steak is fully cooked through.

4. While your beef is cooking, make your slaw. To do this use a medium sized bowl and add in your green and purple cabbage, shredded carrots, fresh lime juice, olive oil and fresh green onions. Toss to combine and season with a dash of salt and black pepper.

5. Place your tortillas onto a flat surface. Fill each of your tortillas with at least ¼ cup of your slaw and top off with an even amount of cooked flank steak. Top off with at least two spoonfuls of your cucumbers. Serve right away and enjoy.

6) Sweet Hawaiian Shrimp

Here is yet another great tasting shrimp dish that I know you are going to want to make as often as possible. It is so delicious even the pickiest of children will be begging you for more.

Serving Size: 6 Servings

Preparation Time: 25 Minutes

Ingredient List:

- 1 Pound of Shrimp, Raw Tail On
- ¼ Cup of Olive Oil, Extra Virgin Variety
- 2 Lemons, Fresh, Juice Only and Evenly Divided
- 5 to 6 Cloves of Garlic, Minced
- 2 Tablespoons of Parsley, Fresh and Roughly Chopped
- 1 tablespoon of Flour, All-Purpose Variety
- ½ teaspoons of Cayenne Pepper, For Taste
- ½ teaspoons of Black Pepper, For Taste
- 6 Tablespoons of Butter, Soft
- 1 teaspoon of Black Pepper, For Taste
- ½ teaspoons of Lemon Zest, Fresh and Optional

Ingredients for Serving:

- Some White Rice, Steamed Variety
- Some Slices of Pineapple, Fresh
- Some Lemon Wedges, Fresh
- Some Lettuce, Fresh and Finely Shredded

zzzzzzzzzzzzzzzzzzzzzzzzzzzzzzzzzzzzzzzzzzzzzzzzzzzzzz

Instructions:

1. First, place a large sized bowl and add in your shrimp. Add in your olive oil, fresh lemon juice, finely chopped garlic, freshly chopped parsley, all-purpose flour, dash of cayenne pepper and black pepper. Stir to thoroughly combine and cover your bowl with a sheet of plastic wrap. Place into your fridge to marinate for at least 30 minutes.

2. Heat place a large sized skillet over medium heat. Once your skillet is hot enough scoop in your shrimp and season with a dash of salt and pepper. Stir thoroughly to combine and add in your garlic. Stir again.

3. Cook your shrimp for the next 2 to 3 minutes on each side or until pink in color. Remove, but leave your garlic in your skillet.

4. Add in your soft butter and some additional pepper. Cook for the next 1 to 4 minutes or until your garlic turns golden brown in color. Remove from heat.

5. Add in your freshly chopped parsley, remaining lemon juice and lemon zest if you are using it.

6. Drizzle this butter mixture over your cooked shrimp and serve with your rice. Garnish with some additional parsley, fresh lemon wedges, shredded lettuce and pineapple slices.

7) Delicious Cheese Steak Quesadillas

Quesadillas are the go to dishes, especially for many picky eaters. They are packed full of protein and cheese to make a dish that will leave you full and satisfied. This particular recipe is so delicious I know it will become highly popular within your household.

Serving Size: 4 Servings

Preparation Time: 30 Minutes

Ingredient List:

- 1 Pound of Beef Steak, Sirloin Variety and Cut into Thin Strips
- 1 Bell Pepper, Red in Color and Sliced Thinly
- 1 Onion, Sliced Thinly
- 2 teaspoons of Salt, Seasoned Variety and Evenly Divided
- 1 teaspoon of Steak Seasoning
- 1 teaspoon of Black Pepper, Evenly Divided and For Taste
- 16 Slices of Provolone Cheese, Sliced Thinly
- 4 Tortillas, Flour Variety and Large in Size
- Some Oil, Canola Variety

ZZZZZZZZZZZZZZZZZZZZZZZZZZZZZZZZZZZZZZZZZZZZZZZZZZZZZZZZZZ

Instructions:

1. Place your steak into a large sized Ziploc bag along with at least one teaspoon of your seasoned salt, steak seasoning and at least half a teaspoon of your black pepper. Shake vigorously until your steak is thoroughly coated.

2. Place a large sized skillet over medium to high heat. Add in a spoonful of your oil and once your oil is hot enough add in your steak. Cook for at least 1 to 2 minutes or until your steak is seared.

3. While your steak is cooking sauté your veggies. To do this use a separate large sized skillet and place over medium heat. Add in a touch of oil and once your oil is hot enough add in your thinly sliced onions and red bell pepper. Season with a dash of salt and black pepper. Cook for at least 8 to 10 minutes or until tender to the touch.

4. Then assemble our quesadillas. To do this place another large sized skillet over medium to high heat. Spray with a generous amount of cooking spray. Place one of your tortillas into it.

5. Layer at least 4 slices of your provolone cheese over your tortilla. Top off with your steak and sautéed veggies. Allow to cook for at least 1 to 2 minutes or until your cheese is melted. Once melted, fold your tortilla over your filling and remove.

6. Repeat with your remaining tortillas and cut into wedges. Serve right away.

8) Asian Style Chicken Wraps

This is a quick and filling recipe that you can make in under 20 minutes. Not only is it incredibly delicious, but it is on the lighter side so you don't have to worry about packing on the pounds in the process.

Serving Size: 4 Servings

Preparation Time: 20 Minutes

Ingredient List:

- 1 tablespoon of Olive Oil, Extra Virgin Variety
- 1 Pound of Chicken, Lean and Ground
- 2 Cloves of Garlic, Minced
- 1 Onion, Large in Size and Finely Diced
- ¼ Cup of Hoisin Sauce
- 2 Tablespoons of Soy Sauce, Your Favorite Kind
- 1 tablespoon of Vinegar, Rice Wine Variety
- 1 tablespoon of Ginger, Freshly Grated
- 1 tablespoon of Sriracha Sauce and Optional
- 1, 8 Ounce Can of Chestnuts, Water Variety, Whole, Drained, Finely Diced and Optional
- 2 Green Onions, Sliced Thinly
- Dash of Salt and Black Pepper, For Taste
- 1 Head of Lettuce, Butter Variety

zzzzzzzzzzzzzzzzzzzzzzzzzzzzzzzzzzzzzzzzzzzzzzzzzzzzzzzzzzzz

Instructions:

1. Place a large sized skillet over medium or high heat. Add in a touch of your olive oil and once your oil is hot enough add in your ground chicken. Cook for the next 5 to 10 minutes or until your chicken is brown in color. As your chicken is cooking, crumble it finely.

2. Drain the excess grease from your chicken and add in your minced garlic, chopped onion, favorite kind of soy sauce, vinegar, freshly grated ginger, dash of Sriracha sauce and hoisin sauce. Stir thoroughly to combine. Continue to cook for the next 1 to 2 minutes or until your onions are soft to the touch and translucent.

3. After this time add in your whole chestnuts if you are using them along with your freshly chopped green onions. Continue to cook for an additional 1 to 2 minutes.

4. Season your mixture with a dash of salt and black pepper. Remove from heat.

5. Spoon a few spoonfuls of your chicken mixture onto your lettuce leaves. Roll taco style and enjoy right away.

9) Drunken Style Aussie Beef Burgers

If you are a huge fan of burgers, then this is one dish I know you will want to make as frequently as possible. Made with a beer spiked beef patty, topped off with some crispy bacon, cheese, onion rings and caramelized pineapple, this is every drunken man's dream.

Serving Size: 4 Servings

Preparation Time: 40 Minutes

Ingredient List:

- 1 Pound of Beef, Extra Lean and Minced
- 2 Cloves of Garlic, Crushed
- 2 Tablespoons of Worcestershire Sauce
- 1/3 Cup of Lager, Your Favorite Kind
- Dash of Salt and Black Pepper, For Taste
- 4 Eggs, Medium in Size
- 4 Slices of Bacon, Fat Removed
- ½ of an Onion, Sliced Thinly
- 4 Slices of Pineapple, Canned Variety
- 1 Handful of Arugula, Fresh
- 8 Slices of Beetroot
- 4 Slices of Cheddar Cheese, Sliced Thinly
- 1 Tomato, Thinly Sliced and Evenly Divided
- 4 Bread Rolls, Cut into Halves
- Some Tomato Sauce, For Serving
- Some Mayonnaise, Your Favorite Kind for Serving and Optional

zzzzzzzzzzzzzzzzzzzzzzzzzzzzzzzzzzzzzzzzzzzzzzzzzzzzzzzz

Instructions:

1. Use a large sized bowl and add in your minced beef, crushed garlic, Worcestershire sauce and favorite kind of lager. Using your hands stir this mixture for at least one minute or until all of the ingredients are incorporated. Divide your meat into 4 equal sized portions and shape into even sized patties.

2. Place a large sized skillet over medium to high heat. Once your skillet is hot enough, add in your patties and sear on both sides until cooked to your desired doneness.

3. While your burgers are cooking, use a separate medium sized skillet and add in a touch of oil. Once your oil is hot enough add in your onion and bacon. Cook for at least 5 minutes or until your onions are translucent and your bacon is crispy to the touch. After this time transfer your bacon and onion onto a large plate lined with paper towels.

4. Wipe your skillet clean and add in a drizzle of oil. Crack your eggs directly into the skillet and fry until the whites of your eggs and yolks are fully set.

5. Transfer your cooked burger patties onto a large sized plate. Wipe clean with a paper towels and add in your pineapple rings. Fry for at least 1 minute on each side or until both sides are well caramelized.

6. Layer the base of your buns with some fresh arugula, your beetroot slices and topped with your freshly cooked burger patties. Layer your cheese, cooked pineapple rings, bacon and onion mixture, fresh tomato slices and fried egg over your cooked burger.

7. Drizzle tomato sauce and mayonnaise over the top and top off with your top portion of your bun. Serve right away and enjoy.

10) Classic Backyard Style Jerk Chicken

Here is yet another New Orleans style chicken dish that you are going to want to enjoy as often as possible. Hearty and packed full of a slight spicy taste, this is one dish that you can make whenever you are looking for something easy to prepare.

Serving Size: 4 Servings

Preparation Time: 40 Minutes

Ingredient List:

- 2 Pounds of Chicken Pieces

Ingredients for Your Marinade:

- 1 Chile, Habanero Variety and Stemmed
- 1 Bunch of Scallions, Cut into Small Sized Pieces
- 2 Cloves of Garlic, Smashed and Peeled
- 1 ½ teaspoons of Thyme, Dried
- 2 Tablespoons of Brown Sugar, Light and Packed
- 1 tablespoon of Allspice, Ground Variety
- 2 Tablespoons of Soy Sauce, Your Favorite Kind
- 2 Tablespoons of Lime Juice, Fresh
- 2 Tablespoons of Oil, Vegetable Variety
- Dash of Salt and Black Pepper, For Taste

ZZZZZZZZZZZZZZZZZZZZZZZZZZZZZZZZZZZZZZZZZZZZZZZZZZZZ

Instructions:

1. The first thing that you will want to do is rinse your chicken thoroughly under some running water. Remove the thigh bones and pat dry with a few paper towels.

2. Then use a food processor and add in all of your ingredients for your marinade. Pulse on the highest setting until smooth in consistency.

3. Use a large sized Ziploc bag and add in your chicken pieces. Pour your marinade over the top and shake to coat. Place into your fridge to marinate overnight.

4. The next day, preheat an outdoor grill to medium or high heat. Once your grill is hot enough remove your chicken from the marinade and place onto your grill. Cook for the next 5 to 8 minutes or until your chicken is golden brown in color and charred on all sides.

5. Remove from your grill and serve right away.

11) Paleo Style Shrimp Tacos

This is the perfect taco recipe to make if you love shrimp. It is crunchy to the taste, packed full of a spicy taste I know you will love and made to perfection, there is no reason not to enjoy these tacos.

Serving Size: 5 Servings

Preparation Time: 25 Minutes

Ingredients for Your Big Bang Sauce:

- 1/3 Cup of Mayonnaise, Your Favorite Kind
- 2 Tablespoons of Chili Sauce, Sweet Variety (Recipe Below)
- 2 Tablespoons of Sriracha

Ingredients for Your Sweet Chili Sauce:

- 3 ½ Tablespoons of Vinegar, White Wine Variety
- 2 Tablespoons of Water, Warm
- 1 ½ Tablespoons of Honey, Raw
- 1 Clove of Garlic, Minced
- 1 teaspoon of Chili Flakes, Crushed
- ½ teaspoons Of Ginger, Minced
- 1/8 teaspoons of Cayenne Pepper
- Dash of Salt, For Taste

Ingredients for Your Tortillas:

- 2 Eggs, Large in Size
- 2/3 Cup of Water, Warm
- 1 Cup of Flour, Tapioca Variety
- ¼ Cup of Flour, Coconut Variety
- ¼ teaspoons of Salt, For Taste

Ingredients for Your Tacos:

- 1 Pound of Shrimp, peeled
- 2 Tablespoons of Flour, Tapioca Variety
- 1/3 Cup of Oil, Coconut Variety and For Frying
- 1 Cup of Cabbage, Napa Variety and Finely Shredded
- ½ Cup of Cabbage, Red in Color and Finely Shredded
- ½ Cup of Cilantro, Fresh and Minced
- 2 Green Onions, Thinly Sliced
- 2 Tablespoons of Olive Oil, Extra Virgin Variety
- 1 tablespoon of Vinegar, White Wine Variety
- ½ Tablespoons of Honey, Raw
- Dash of Salt, For Taste

ZZZZZZZZZZZZZZZZZZZZZZZZZZZZZZZZZZZZZZZZZZZZZZZZZZZZ

Instructions:

1. First make your sweet chili sauce. To do this add all of your ingredients for your chili sauce into a small sized saucepan set over medium heat. Stir thoroughly to combine and bring this mixture to a boil. Once boiling reduce the heat to low and allow to simmer for the next 5 to 10 minutes or until thick in consistency.

2. Remove from heat and allow your mixture to cool before adding in your favorite kind of mayonnaise and Sriracha.

3. Next use a large sized bowl and add in your napa and red cabbage into it along with your cilantro and sliced green onions. Add in at least two spoonfuls of your olive oil, at least one spoonful of your vinegar, at least half a spoonful of your honey and a dash of salt. Toss thoroughly to combine. Set this mixture aside for later use.

4. Then make your tortillas. To do this use a medium sized bowl and add in all of your ingredients for your tortillas into it. Whisk thoroughly until smooth in consistency.

5. Place a large sized cast iron skillet over high heat. Add in a touch of your oil into it and pour in at least 1/5 of your tortillas batter into it, making sure to spread it into a medium sized circle. Allow to cook for at least 1 to 2 minutes before flipping. Continue to cook for another 2 to 3 minutes or until both sides are gold brown in color. Repeat with your remaining batter until all of your tortillas have been made.

6. Place another large sized skillet over high heat. Add in your coconut oil and once your oil is completely melted add in your shrimp and tapioca. Toss thoroughly to combine. Fry for at least 2 minutes or until golden in color. Flip and continue to fry for another 2 to 3 minutes or until your shrimp is fully cooked through.

7. Add your shrimp to your Big bang sauce and toss until thoroughly coated.

8. Place a spoonful of your shrimp into one of your tortillas. Top off with your homemade slaw and a drizzle of Sriracha. Serve right away and enjoy.

12) Philly Style Cheesecake with Garlic Aioli Sauce

Why would you overpay for a Philly cheesecake whenever you can make this delicious dish right from the comfort of your own home. With the help of this recipe, you never have to skimp on a hearty and cheesy meal ever again.

Serving Size: 4 Servings

Preparation Time: 25 Minutes

Ingredient List:

- ¼ Cup of Mayonnaise, Your Favorite Kind
- 2 Cloves of Garlic, Pressed
- 2 Tablespoons of Butter, Soft
- 1 Pound of Chuck Steak, Boneless and Sliced Thinly
- Dash of Salt and Black Pepper, For Taste
- 1 Onion, Sliced Thinly
- 1 Bell Pepper, Red in Color and Thinly Sliced
- 1 Bell Pepper, Green in Color and Thinly Sliced
- 4 Hoagie Rolls, Lightly Toasted and For Serving
- 1 Cup of Cheddar Cheese, White in Color and Finely Shredded

zzzzzzzzzzzzzzzzzzzzzzzzzzzzzzzzzzzzzzzzzzzzzzzzzzzzzzzz

Instructions:

1. The first thing that you will want to do is preheat your oven to broil.

2. While your oven is broiling make your garlic aioli sauce. To do this, use a small sized bowl and add in your favorite kind or mayonnaise and your pressed garlic. Whisk thoroughly until smooth in consistency.

3. Place a medium sized cast iron skillet over medium to high heat. Add in your butter and once your butter is fully melted add in your chuck steak. Cook for the next 5 to 6 minutes or until your steak is medium rare. Season your steak with a dash of salt and black pepper and set aside for later use.

4. Add your chopped onions and green and red bell peppers into your skillet. Cook for the next 5 to 6 minutes or until tender to the touch and golden in color.

5. Next assemble your sandwiches. To do this spread your garlic aioli sauce inside your rolls. Top off with your cooked steak, tender onions and bell pepper. Sprinkle your shredded cheddar cheese over the top and place onto a large sized baking sheet.

6. Place into your oven to bake for the next 2 minutes or until your cheese is fully melted. Remove and serve immediately.

13) Truck Stop Enchiladas

One of the things that most truck stops are renowned for is the fact that most of the food served happens to be some of the most delicious that you will ever find. The same holds true with these enchiladas as they happen to be the most delicious enchiladas that you will ever come across.

Serving Size: 6 Servings

Preparation Time: 35 Minutes

Ingredient List:

- 12 Tortillas, Corn Variety
- 1 Pound of Cheddar Cheese, Mild Variety and Finely Shredded
- 2, 8 Ounce Cans of Chile Con Carne
- 1 Onion, Small in Size and Finely Chopped
- Some Oil, Vegetable Variety and For Cooking
- Dash of Cilantro, Fresh, Roughly Chopped and For Garnish

zzzzzzzzzzzzzzzzzzzzzzzzzzzzzzzzzzzzzzzzzzzzzzzzzzzzz

Instructions:

1. Pour in at least ¼ inch of oil into a large sized skillet placed over medium heat. Once your oil begins to smoke dip a tortilla into it. Fry for at least 5 seconds before flipping and continuing to fry for another 5 minutes more.

2. Heat up your cans of chile con carne in a separate skillet placed over medium heat. Once hot to the touch, dip your tortillas into it. Move your tortillas to a large sized greased baking dish.

3. Place at least 2 spoonfuls of your shredded cheese into your tortillas and roll. Place the seam side facing down. Repeat with your remaining tortillas.

4. Sprinkle your cheese over the top and pour your remaining chile con carne over the top as well. Top off with some onion and a last layer of shredded cheese.

5. Next preheat your oven to 400 degrees. Once your oven is hot enough, add in your enchiladas and cook for the next 10 minutes or until your cheese is fully melted.

6. Remove and serve immediately with a garnish of cilantro.

14) Sweet Apple Pie Tacos

This is a classic and delicious twist on a traditional taco recipe that I know you are going to love. It is a great way to satisfy those picky eaters in your household as well as satisfy your own strong sweet tooth in the process. For the best results, make this during the holiday season to really get into the spirit.

Serving Size: 6 Servings

Preparation Time: 10 Minutes

Ingredients for Your Taco Shells:

- 6 Tortillas, Flour Variety
- Some Oil, Vegetable Variety and For Frying
- 2/3 Cup of Sugar, White in Color
- 2 teaspoons of Cinnamon, Ground

Ingredients for Your Filling:

- 1, 21 Ounce Can of Pie Filling, Apple Variety and Chopped

Other Ingredient List:

- Some Whipped Topping, Frozen and For Serving
- Some Caramel Sauce, For Topping and Store-Bought Variety

ZZZZZZZZZZZZZZZZZZZZZZZZZZZZZZZZZZZZZZZZZZZZZZZZZZZZZZZ

Instructions:

1. First, use a circle cutter that is at least 3 ½ inches in diameter and cut out circles from your tortillas.

2. Then use a small sized bowl and add in your white sugar and ground cinnamon. Set aside for later use.

3. Pour in at least 1 ½ inch of oil into a large sized pot set over medium heat. Once your oil begins to bubble, add in a circle of your tortillas. Allow to fry for at least 5 seconds before flipping. Use a pair of tongs and fold over one side of the tortilla and hold it while it is folded until brown in color. Flip again and continue to fry until crispy. Remove and shake to get rid of the excess oil. Roll immediately in your cinnamon and sugar mixture. Set aside to cool until you are ready to use them.

4. While your taco shells are cooling pour your apple pie filling into a medium sized saucepan set over medium heat. Cook for at least 1 to 3 minutes or until piping hot.

5. Fill each of your taco shells with at least two spoonfuls of your apple pie filling. Top off with your whipped topping and drizzle your caramel sauce over the top. Serve warm for the best results.

15) Asian Burgers with Sriracha Mayo Sauce

If you have been looking for a way to spice up your burgers, then this is the perfect dish for you to put together. These particular burgers are incredibly delicious and contain a touch of spice that I know you won't be able to resist.

Serving Size: 4 Servings

Preparation Time: 25 Minutes

Ingredients for Your Burgers:

- 1 ½ Pound of Beef, Lean and Ground
- ¼ Cup of Breadcrumbs, Panko Variety
- 2 Tablespoons of Oyster Sauce, Asian Variety
- 2 Tablespoons of Soy Sauce, Your Favorite Kind
- 1 tablespoon of Sugar, Granulated Variety
- 2 teaspoons of Garlic, Powdered Variety
- 2 teaspoons of Onion, Powdered Variety
- 1 teaspoon of Sesame Oil, Asian Variety and Lightly Toasted
- ½ teaspoons of Ginger, Ground
- ¼ teaspoons of Pepper, White in Color
- ¼ teaspoons of Salt, For Taste
- 1 Egg, Large in Size

Ingredients for Your Sriracha Mayo:

- ½ Cup of Mayonnaise, Whole and Your Favorite Kind
- 4 teaspoons of Sriracha Sauce
- 2 Tablespoons of Mustard, Dijon Variety

Ingredients for Serving:

- 3 Ciabatta Rolls, Fresh
- 8 Ounces of Coleslaw, Your Favorite Kind
- Some Cilantro, Whole Leaves and Fresh

ZZZZZZZZZZZZZZZZZZZZZZZZZZZZZZZZZZZZZZZZZZZZZZZZZZZZZZZ

Instructions:

1. First make your sriracha mayonnaise. To do this use a medium sized bowl and add in your favorite kind of mayonnaise, sriracha sauce and Dijon style mustard. Whisk until thoroughly combined.

2. Then use a large sized bowl and add in all of your ingredients for your burgers into it. Stir thoroughly to combine. Then use your hands and form your mixture into patties.

3. Preheat an outdoor grill or indoor griddle to medium or high heat. Once hot enough, add in your burgers and grill for at least 5 to 10 minutes or cooked to your desired doneness. Remove and place onto your ciabatta rolls.

4. Top off with your fresh coleslaw, cilantro leaves and a drizzle of sriracha mayo over the top. Serve immediately and enjoy.

16) Delicious Crab and Brie Grilled Cheese Sandwich

Once you get a taste of this delicious dish for yourself, I can guarantee that you will never want to enjoy boring traditional grilled cheese sandwiches again. Packed full of crab and brie, this is one dish that every seafood lover with fall in love with.

Serving Size: 2 Servings

Preparation Time: 8 Minutes

Ingredient List:

- 1 Cup of Crab Meat, Dungeness Variety
- 2 Tablespoons of Mayonnaise, Your Favorite Kind
- 1 Lemon, Fresh, Zest and Juice Only
- 1 tablespoon of Chives, Freshly Chopped
- 4 Dashes of Tabasco Sauce
- 4 Slices of Bread, Artisan Variety and Thick Cut
- 4 Tablespoons of Cheese, Mascarpone Variety
- ¼ Cup of Cheddar Cheese, Finely Shredded
- 1 Tomato, Fresh and Finely Diced
- ¼ Cup of Cucumber, Thinly Sliced
- 4 Slices of Brie
- 4 Tablespoons of Mango Chutney
- 2 Tablespoons of Butter, Soft
- Dash of Black Pepper Freshly Cracked and For Taste
- 1 Lemon, Fresh and For Garnish

ZZZZZZZZZZZZZZZZZZZZZZZZZZZZZZZZZZZZZZZZZZZZZZZZZZZZZZZZZ

Instructions:

1. Use a large sized bowl and add in your fresh crab meat, favorite kind of mayonnaise, fresh lemon juice, fresh lemon zest, chopped chives and Tabasco sauce. Stir thoroughly to combine and set aside for later use.

2. Place a large sized skillet over medium heat and add in your butter. Allow to heat up for the next 45 seconds or until it begins to foam.

3. Place your bread onto a large sized baking sheet. Preheat your oven to 350 degrees and once your oven is hot enough add in your bread. Bake for at least 4 minutes or until golden brown in color.

4. Garnish your bread with a touch of lemon and dash of black pepper. Top off with your slices of mascarpone cheese, shredded cheddar cheese, your crab mixture, chopped tomato, freshly sliced cucumber, brie, mango chutney and finely top off with your bread. Serve right away and enjoy.

17) Vietnamese Style Banh Mi Street Tacos

With the help of this delicious taco recipe you don't have to travel across the world just to enjoy it. These tacos are not only incredibly easy to make, but they are surprisingly nutritious for you as well.

Serving Size: 20 Servings

Preparation Time: 30 Minutes

Ingredients for Your Banh Mi Chicken:

- 2 Tablespoons of Oil, Coconut Variety
- 2 Pounds of Chicken Thighs, Skinless and Boneless Variety
- ½ Cup of Lime Juice, Fresh
- 1/3 Cup of Fish Sauce
- ¼ Cup of Sugar, Granulated Variety
- 1 Jalapeno Pepper, Sliced Thinly
- 4 Cloves of Garlic, Minced

Ingredients for Your Spicy Mayo:

- ¾ Cup of Mayonnaise, Your Favorite Kind
- 1 to 2 Tablespoons of Sriracha
- 1 tablespoon of Vinegar, Rice Variety
- 1 tablespoon of Sugar, Granulated Variety

Ingredients for Your Tacos:

- 2 Packs of Tortillas, El Paso Variety, Flour Variety and Taco Size
- 3 Carrots, Fresh and Finely Shredded
- 1 Cucumber, English Variety and Sliced Thinly
- 2 Bunches of Radishes, Sliced Thinly
- 4 Jalapeños, Sliced Thinly
- 1 Bunch of Cilantro, Fresh and Roughly Chopped
- 2 Limes, Fresh and Cut into Wedges

ZZZZZZZZZZZZZZZZZZZZZZZZZZZZZZZZZZZZZZZZZZZZZZZZZZZZZZZZZZZ

Instructions:

1. The first thing that you will want to do is make your chicken. To do this, use a medium sized bowl that is microwave safe and add in your fish sauce, fresh lime juice and granulated sugar. Place into your microwave and cook for the next 1 to 2 minutes or until your sugar fully dissolves.

2. Next cut your chicken into small sized pieces and add into your bowl along with your sliced jalapeño and minced garlic. Stir thoroughly to combine and transfer into your fridge to chill for the next hour.

3. While your chicken is chilling, make your spicy mayo. To do this use a small sized bowl that is microwave safe and add in your sugar and rice style vinegar. Stir to combine and place into your microwave to cook for the next minute or until your sugar is fully dissolved. Add in your favorite kind of mayonnaise and sriracha sauce. Stir to incorporate and place into your fridge to chill until ready for use.

4. Drain your chicken from the marinade. Then place a large sized skillet over medium to high heat. Add in a spoonful of coconut oil and once your oil is hot enough add in your chicken. Sear for at least 4 to 5 minutes or until caramelized on all sides. Remove from heat.

5. Place a scoop of your chicken into the middle of your flour tortillas. Top off with your freshly shredded carrots, cucumber, fresh radishes, cilantro and jalapeño slices. Drizzle your spicy mayo over the top and serve with your fresh lime wedges. Serve right away and enjoy.

18) Deep Fried S'mores

If You are looking for a dish that will help to satisfy your strongest sweet tooth, then this is the perfect sweet dish for you to make. Packed full of that sweet s'mores taste that you love, I guarantee that you will never want to make traditional s'mores again.

Serving Size: 36 Servings

Preparation Time: 40 Minutes

Ingredient List:

- 9 Graham Cracker Sheets
- 2 Chocolate Bars, Extra Large Variety
- ½ Cup of Chocolate Chips, Milk Variety
- 20 to 24 Marshmallows, Large in Size
- 1 Egg, Large in Size
- 1 teaspoon of Oil, Vegetable Variety
- ¾ Cup of Milk, Whole
- 1 Cup + 2 Tablespoons of Flour, All-Purpose Variety
- 3 Tablespoons of Sugar, Granulated Variety
- ½ teaspoons of Baker's Style Baking Powder
- 1/8 teaspoons of Salt, For Taste
- 1 Quart of Oil, Vegetable Variety

ZZZZZZZZZZZZZZZZZZZZZZZZZZZZZZZZZZZZZZZZZZZZZZZZZZZZZZZ

Instructions:

1. First line a large sized baking pan with a sheet of plastic wrap. Place your graham cracker sheets into the bottom of your pan.

2. Then use a small sized saucepan and set over low heat. Add in your chocolate chips and cook for the next 3 minutes or until thoroughly melted. Spread at least 1/3 of your chocolate chips on top of your graham crackers. Top off with your chocolate bars and finely your large sized marshmallows.

3. Spread a thin layer of your melted chocolate chips over your marshmallows. Add a final layer of your graham crackers.

4. Place this mixture into your fridge to chill for the next couple of minutes or until your chocolate is set.

5. While your s'mores are chilling make your batter. To do this, use a small sized bowl and add in your egg, oil and whole milk. Whisk to combine. Then use a separate medium sized bowl and add in your flour, white sugar, baker's style baking powder and dash of salt. Stir to combine and add to your wet ingredients. Whisk until your batter is smooth in consistency.

6. Once your chocolate has set cut your s'mores into 36 even sized pieces.

7. Then pour at least 2 inches of oil into a medium sized saucepan placed over medium to high heat. Heat your oil until it reaches 375 degrees.

8. While your oil is heating up take one piece of your s'more and dip into your batter. Gently drop into your oil and repeat until all of your s'mores have been coated. Fry for at least 2 minutes or until golden brown in color. Remove and place onto a plate lined with a few paper towels. Repeat with your remaining s'more until all have been fried. Serve immediately.

19) Easy Buttermilk Fried Chicken

If you love the taste of classic fried chicken, then this is the perfect food truck dish for you to make. Incredibly juicy and tender on the inside and perfectly crispy on the outside, I know you won't be able to get enough of this chicken.

Serving Size: 4 Servings

Preparation Time: 45 Minutes

Ingredient List:

- 2 Cups of Buttermilk, Whole
- 2 Eggs, Large in Size
- 1 teaspoon of Paprika
- 1 teaspoon of Hot Sauce, Your Favorite Kind
- Dash of Salt and Pepper, For Taste
- 2 teaspoons of Baker's Style Baking Powder
- 1 ½ teaspoons of Baker's Style Baking Soda
- Some Flour, For Dreding
- 1 Pound of Chicken Breasts, Skinless and Boneless Preferable
- Some Oil, Vegetable Variety and For Frying

ZZZZZZZZZZZZZZZZZZZZZZZZZZZZZZZZZZZZZZZZZZZZZZZZZZZZZZZ

Instructions:

1. The first thing that you will want to do is wash your chicken thoroughly under some water. Pat dry with a few paper towels.

2. Then use a large sized bowl and add in your whole buttermilk, large eggs, paprika, your favorite kind of hot sauce and a dash of salt and black pepper. Whisk thoroughly until thoroughly combined.

3. Use another large sized bowl and add in your baker's style baking soda and powder. Stir to combine and add this mixture to your liquid mixture. Whisk again until smooth in consistency and foamy.

4. Place enough flour for dredging into a large sized shallow dish.

5. Dredge your chicken on all sides in your flour. Dip into your buttermilk mixture and dredge back in your flour. Repeat with your remaining chicken.

6. Place a large sized frying pan over medium heat and pour in at least an inch of oil. Once your oil is piping hot gently drop in your chicken. Fry for at least 3 to 5 minutes or until your chicken is golden in color. Flip and continue to fry for an additional 3 to 5 minutes or until golden in color on the other side. Remove and place onto a large sized plate lined with paper towels to drain. Repeat with your remaining chicken until all has been fried.

7. Serve while still warm and enjoy.

20) New Orleans Style Food Truck Fries

Once you get a taste of these fries for yourself, I guarantee that you will never want to enjoy any other fry recipe again. Packed full of an authentic New Orleans taste, this is one fry dish I know you won't be able to get enough of.

Serving Size: 4 Servings

Preparation Time: 45 Minutes

Ingredient List:

- 4 Potatoes, Russet Variety, Washed and Cut into Thin Strips
- ¼ Cup of Parsley, Fresh and Roughly Chopped
- 1/3 Cup of Parmesan Cheese, Freshly Grated
- 2 Tablespoons of Oil, Vegetable Variety
- 2 teaspoons of Creole Seasoning

zzzzzzzzzzzzzzzzzzzzzzzzzzzzzzzzzzzzzzzzzzzzzzzzzzzzzzzzzzzzz

Instructions:

1. The first thing that you will want to do is preheat your oven to 400 degrees.

2. While your oven is heating up cut your potatoes into thin strips. Then place into a bowl of water to soak for at least 15 to 20 minutes before draining. Pat dry with a few paper towels.

3. Using a large sized baking sheet lined with a sheet of parchment paper, add in your potato strips, creole seasoning and vegetable oil. Toss to coat thoroughly.

4. Place into your oven to bake for the next 20 minutes, making sure to flip as it bakes until brown in color.

5. Remove from your oven after this time, and toss your freshly made fries with some freshly grated Parmesan cheese and chopped parsley. Toss to thoroughly coat.

6. Serve these fries with some mayo and ketchup. Enjoy!

21) Cheesy Bacon Wrapped Hot Dogs

If you are a huge fan of hot dogs, then this is one delicious and unique hot dog recipe I know you are going to want to make over and over again. These are the perfect hot dogs to make during the fourth of July to celebrate the holiday.

Serving Size: 8 Servings

Preparation Time: 15 Minutes

Ingredient List:

- 8 Hot Dogs, Your Favorite Kind
- American Cheese 3 Slices, Cut into Thin Strips
- 16 Slices of Bacon, Fully Cooked
- 8 Hot Dog Buns, Your Favorite Kind

ZZZZZZZZZZZZZZZZZZZZZZZZZZZZZZZZZZZZZZZZZZZZZZZZZZZZZZZZZ

Instructions:

1. First preheat your oven to 450 degrees.

2. While your oven is heating up slice your hotdogs directly down the middle. Stuff your hotdog with your strips of American cheese.

3. Wrap a slice of bacon around your hot dog and secure in place with a toothpick.

4. Place your hotdogs onto a large sized baking sheet and place into your oven to bake for the next 10 minutes.

5. Remove from your oven and remove your toothpicks. Serve your hotdogs onto your hot dog buns and enjoy right away.

22) Korean Style BBQ Short Rib Dogs with a Sweet Peach Relish

While at first you may assume that this dish is a hot dog dish, you will be pleasantly surprised when you begin to put it together. Made with tangy short ribs and a sweet relish, this is the perfect dish to make during Memorial Day weekend.

Serving Size: 8 Servings

Preparation Time: 4 Hours and 30 Minutes

Ingredients for Your Korean BBQ Short Rib Dogs:

- 5 Pounds of Short Ribs, Bone in Variety
- ¾ Cup of Brown Sugar, Light and Packed
- 1 Cup of Soy Sauce, 3 Tablespoons Set Aside and Evenly Divided
- ½ Cup of Water, Warm
- 1/3 Cup of Vinegar, Rice Wine Variety
- 4 Green Onions, Finely Chopped
- 2 Cloves of Garlic, Minced
- ½ Tablespoons of Ginger, Freshly Grated
- 2 Tablespoons of Sesame Oil, Lightly Toasted
- ½ teaspoons of Black Pepper, For Taste
- 6 Tablespoons of Korean Chile Paste
- ½ Cup of Ketchup
- 4 to 6 Hoagie Buns, Whole Wheat Variety
- 4 to 6 Ounces of Swiss Cheese, Finely Shredded
- 2 to 4 Ounces of Feta Cheese, Crumbled

Ingredients for Your Korean Chile Slaw:

- 3 Cups of Cabbage, Green in Color, Fresh and Finely Shredded
- 1 Cup of Carrot, Cut into Small Matchsticks
- ½ Cup of Cilantro, Fresh and Roughly Chopped
- 2 Green Onions, Finely Chopped
- 1 Lime, Juice Only
- 2 Tablespoons of Soy Sauce, Your Favorite Kind
- 1 tablespoon of Vinegar, Rice Wine Variety
- 1 to 2 Tablespoons of Korean Chile Paste
- 1 tablespoon of Oil, Sesame Variety and Lightly Toasted
- 2 Tablespoons of Sesame Seeds, Lightly Toasted

Ingredients for Your Sweet Peach Relish:

- 2 Peaches, Fresh and Finely Chopped
- 1 Jalapeno Pepper, Seeded and Finely Chopped
- ¼ Cup of Cilantro, Fresh and Roughly Chopped
- 1 Lime, Juice Only

zzzzzzzzzzzzzzzzzzzzzzzzzzzzzzzzzzzzzzzzzzzzzzzzzzzzzzzz

Instructions:

1. The first thing that you will want to do is prepare your ribs. To do this, place your ribs into a gallox sized Ziploc bag.

2. Then use a large sized bowl and add in your brown sugar, at least one cup of your soy sauce, warm water, vinegar, chopped green onions, minced garlic, freshly grated ginger, lightly toasted sesame oil and dash of black pepper. Stir thoroughly to combine and pour this mixture over your ribs. Seal your bag and place into your fridge to marinate for the next 4 hours.

3. Next preheat your oven to 325 degrees.

4. After your ribs have marinated, place into a large sized roasting pan. Cover with a sheet of aluminum foil and place into your oven to bake for the next 2 ½ hours or until your ribs are tender to the touch.

5. After your ribs have finished baking strain the cooking liquid into a medium sized saucepan. Add in your chile paste and ketchup. Place over medium heat and bring this mixture to a boil. Boil for at least 10 minutes or until reduced by at least half and thick in consistency. Remove from heat.

6. Next preheat an outdoor grill to medium or high heat.

7. Brush your ribs with your barbecue sauce and place directly onto your preheated grill. Grill for the next 7 to 8 minutes on each side. Remove from your grill and allow to cool for the next 5 minutes before shredding the meat off of the bone using two forks.

8. Next, make your Korean style chili slaw. To do this, use a large sized bowl and add in your green cabbage, carrot matchsticks, roughly chopped cilantro and chopped green onions. Toss to combine. Then use a separate medium sized bowl and add in your fresh lime juice, favorite kind of soy sauce, chile paste, oil and toasted sesame seeds. Whisk thoroughly to combine and place into your fridge until you are ready to use it.

9. Then make your peach relish. To do this, use a medium sized bowl and add in your freshly chopped peaches, sliced jalapenos, roughly chopped cilantro and fresh lime juice. Stir thoroughly to combine.

10. Stuff your rib meat into your buns. Top off with some Swiss cheese, your freshly made peach relish and coleslaw. Sprinkle the top with some feta cheese and serve right away.

23) Savory Fried Chicken Sliders with Buffalo Sauce

These little sliders are so delicious, even the pickiest of eaters won't be able to resist it. Made with savory fried chicken and smothered in a spicy buffalo sauce, I know you won't be able to get enough of these tiny burgers.

Serving Size: 12 Servings

Preparation Time: 37 Minutes

Ingredients for Your Marinade:

- 2 Chicken Breasts, Large in Size
- 1 ½ Cups of Buttermilk, Whole
- ¼ Cup of Buffalo Sauce, Your Favorite Kind
- ½ Tablespoons of Salt, Garlic Variety

Ingredients for Your Dry Mixture:

- 1 ½ Cups of Flour, All-Purpose Variety
- ¼ teaspoons of Salt, For Taste
- ½ teaspoons of Onion, Powdered Variety
- Dash of Black Pepper, For Taste
- 1 tablespoon of Herbs de Provence
- 1 teaspoon of Paprika, Smoked Variety

Ingredients for Serving:

- 12 Slider Buns, Miniature Variety
- 6 Slices of Pepper Jack Cheese, Cut into Halves
- 5 Cups of Oil, Canola Variety

zzzzzzzzzzzzzzzzzzzzzzzzzzzzzzzzzzzzzzzzzzzzzzzzzzzzzzzzzzzz

Instructions:

1. First, slice your chicken breast into 6 equal sized pieces. Then transfer your chicken into a large sized bowl along with your whole buttermilk, buffalo sauce and dash of garlic salt. Stir thoroughly until your chicken is fully coated.

2. Cover your chicken with a sheet of plastic wrap and allow to marinate for the next 4 hours.

3. Meanwhile use a separate medium sized bowl and add in your all-purpose flour, dash of salt, powdered onion, dash of black pepper, herbs de Provence and smoked paprika. Stir thoroughly to combine.

4. Pour your oil into a large sized pot and set over medium heat. Heat up your oil until it reaches 375 degrees. Once your oil is hot enough gently dredge your chicken in your flour mixture and drop into your hot oil. Fry for at least 3 minutes on each side or until your chicken is fully cooked through. Remove and transfer to a plate lined with paper towels to drain.

5. Season your chicken with a dash of salt.

6. Place your chicken onto your miniature slider buns and top off with a half slice of cheese. Drizzle some more buffalo sauce over the top and serve right away.

24) Food Truck Style Mac and Cheese

There is no other mac and cheese recipe quite as delicious as this one. Once you get a bite of it yourself, I guarantee that you will want to make it over and over again. Feel free to top off with more cheese for the tastiest results.

Serving Size: 8 to 10 Servings

Preparation Time: 40 Minutes

Ingredient List:

- 8 Ounces of Macaroni, Elbow Variety
- 1 tablespoon of Milk, Dry and Nonfat Variety
- 2 Tablespoons of Flour, All-Purpose Variety
- 1 tablespoon of Butter, Fully Melted
- 1 ¼ Cup of Water, Boiling
- 3 Cups of American Cheese, Freshly Grated
- ¼ teaspoons of Salt, For Taste

zzzzzzzzzzzzzzzzzzzzzzzzzzzzzzzzzzzzzzzzzzzzzzzzzzzzzzzz

Instructions:

1. The first thing that you will want to do, is cook up your macaroni according to the directions on the package. Once your macaroni is tender to the touch drain and set aside for later use.

2. Next preheat your oven to 350 degrees.

3. While your oven is heating up, use a large sized bowl and add in your dried milk, all-purpose flour and fully melted butter. Gently add in your boiling water and beat thoroughly until smooth in consistency. Add in at least 1 ½ cup of your grated cheese, making sure to beat again until creamy in consistency.

4. Add in your cooked macaroni and fold gently to incorporate. Add in your remaining cheese and season with a dash of salt.

5. Transfer this mixture into a large sized baking dish. Cover with a sheet of aluminum foil and place into your oven to bake for an additional 25 minutes.

6. Remove from your oven after this time and remove your sheet of aluminum foil. Serve while still piping hot and enjoy.

25) Vietnamese Style Caramel Shrimp Sandwich

This is yet another delicious shrimp recipe that you can make if you are craving shrimp tonight. It makes for a filling dish to make that can be ready on your table in just a matter of minutes.

Serving Size: 4 Servings

Preparation Time: 20 Minutes

Ingredient List:

- 1 Baguette, French Variety and Cut Into 4 Equal Sized Pieces
- 4 Tablespoons of Mayonnaise, Your Favorite Kind
- 1 Pound of Shrimp, Caramelized and Recipe Below
- ¼ Cup of Daikon Radish, Pickled Variety
- ¼ Cup of Carrots, Pickled Variety
- ½ Cup of Cucumber, Fresh and Sliced Thinly
- ½ Cup of Cilantro, Fresh and Roughly Chopped
- 2 Chilies, Birds Eye Variety, Thinly Sliced and Optional
- Dash of Soy Sauce, For Taste

Ingredients for Your Caramel Shrimp:

- 2 Tablespoons of Sugar, White in Color
- 4 Tablespoons of Water, Warm
- 1 tablespoon of Oil, Canola Variety
- 1 Shallot, Diced Finely
- 2 Cloves of Garlic, Finely Chopped
- 1 Pound of Shrimp, Peeled and Deveined
- 1 tablespoon of Fish Sauce
- Dash of Black Pepper, For Taste

ZZZZZZZZZZZZZZZZZZZZZZZZZZZZZZZZZZZZZZZZZZZZZZZZZZZZZZZ

Instructions:

1. First make your shrimp. To do this, place a large sized skillet over medium to high heat. Add in your sugar and warm water. Stir thoroughly to combine and cook for the next 15 minutes or until your sugar caramelizes and is dark brown in color. Remove from heat and set aside for later use.

2. Place a separate large sized skillet over medium heat. Add in a touch of oil and once your oil is hot enough add in your shallots and chopped garlic. Stir thoroughly to combine and cook for the next 3 to 5 minutes.

3. After this time add in your shrimp, premade caramel sauce, fish sauce and black pepper. Stir thoroughly to combine and cook for the next 2 to 3 minutes or until your shrimp is pink in color.

4. Next assemble your sandwiches. To do this, place your shrimp into the middle of your baguette rolls. Top off with your favorite kind of mayonnaise, fresh daikon radish, picked carrots, thinly sliced cucumbers, chopped cilantro, chilies if you are using them and a dash of your soy sauce.

5. Repeat with your remaining baguette pieces and enjoy right away.

About the Author

A native of Albuquerque, New Mexico, Sophia Freeman found her calling in the culinary arts when she enrolled at the Sante Fe School of Cooking. Freeman decided to take a year after graduation and travel around Europe, sampling the cuisine from small bistros and family owned restaurants from Italy to Portugal. Her bubbly personality and inquisitive nature made her popular with the locals in the villages and when she finished her trip and came home, she had made friends for life in the places she had visited. She also came home with a deeper understanding of European cuisine.

Freeman went to work at one of Albuquerque's 5-star restaurants as a sous-chef and soon worked her way up to head chef. The restaurant began to feature Freeman's original dishes as specials on the menu and soon after, she began to write e-books with her recipes. Sophia's dishes mix local flavours with European inspiration making them irresistible to the diners in her restaurant and the online community.

Freeman's experience in Europe didn't just teach her new ways of cooking, but also unique methods of presentation. Using rich sauces, crisp vegetables and meat cooked to perfection, she creates a stunning display as well as a delectable dish. She has won many local awards for her cuisine and she continues to delight her diners with her culinary masterpieces.

Author's Afterthoughts

I want to convey my big thanks to all of my readers who have taken the time to read my book. Readers like you make my work so rewarding and I cherish each and every one of you.

Grateful cannot describe how I feel when I know that someone has chosen my work over all of the choices available online. I hope you enjoyed the book as much as I enjoyed writing it.

Feedback from my readers is how I grow and learn as a chef and an author. Please take the time to let me know your thoughts by leaving a review on Amazon so I and your fellow readers can learn from your experience.

My deepest thanks,

Sophia Freeman

https://sophia.subscribemenow.com/

Made in the USA
Monee, IL
24 February 2020